GREAT STORYTELLERS

CHRISTOPHER PAUL CURTIS

Erinn Banting

www.openlightbox.com

Step 1
Go to **www.openlightbox.com**

Step 2
Enter this unique code
QZGONPN48

Step 3
Explore your interactive eBook!

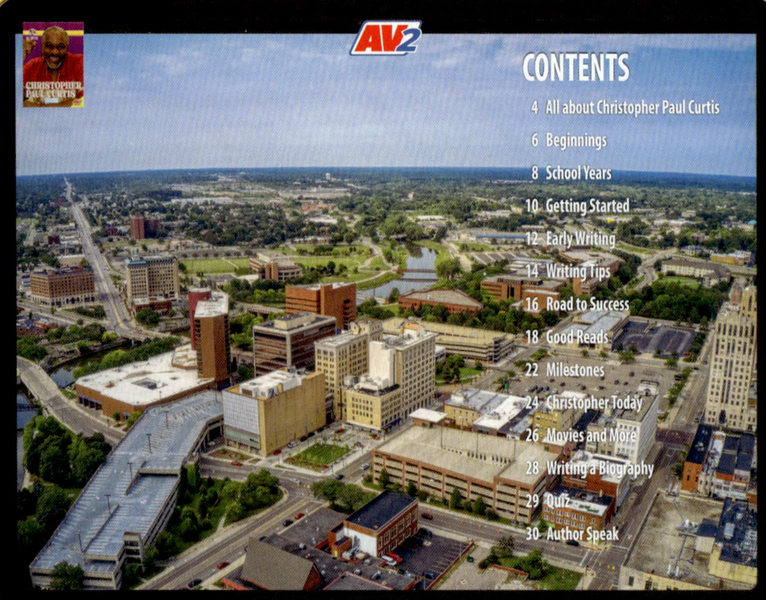

AV2 is optimized for use on any device

Your interactive eBook comes with...

Contents
Browse a live contents page to easily navigate through resources

Audio
Listen to sections of the book read aloud

Videos
Watch informative video clips

Weblinks
Gain additional information for research

Slideshows
View images and captions

Try This!
Complete activities and hands-on experiments

Key Words
Study vocabulary, and complete a matching word activity

Quizzes
Test your knowledge

Share
Share titles within your Learning Management System (LMS) or Library Circulation System

Citation
Create bibliographical references following APA, CMOS, and MLA styles

Contents

All about Christopher Paul Curtis

Christopher Paul Curtis is an award-winning children's writer. A vivid storyteller, Christopher writes about difficult subjects, such as **slavery**. Many of his stories take place during challenging periods in history. They often focus on the importance of family. Christopher uses humor and pain to create characters that resonate with readers.

Christopher worked hard to become a writer. His first book was published when he was 42 years old. Since then, he has written powerful books that children around the world love to read.

When Christopher first began writing, he did not intend to be a children's author. The stories he wanted to tell just sounded better when told from a child's point of view.

Christopher's books have been translated into more than **10 languages.**

The **first** book Christopher had published sold more than **3 million copies.**

Beginnings

Christopher was born on May 10, 1953, in Flint, Michigan. He is the second of five children. His father, Herman, was a chiropodist, or foot doctor. His mother, Leslie Jane, was a teacher. When her children were small, she stayed home and took care of them. When they were older, she became the first person to teach Black history in their area.

Herman's job as a chiropodist did not pay enough to support a growing family. As more children arrived, it became difficult to make ends meet. When Christopher was 3 years old, Herman went to work at the General Motors car factory in Flint. Working at the factory gave Herman a stable income and allowed him to provide for his wife and children.

Herman and Leslie Jane were both avid readers. Every Saturday, Herman took his children to the library. Christopher read books in school, but he did not enjoy reading on his own. He noticed that there were not many books written by African Americans. He wanted to read stories about people like him, by people like him.

More than 80,000 people live in Flint, Michigan. Flint's nickname is "Vehicle City" because it has been producing vehicles, ranging from carriages to cars, since the late 19th century.

Where Christopher Was Born

Lake Superior
CANADA
UNITED STATES
Lake Huron
Lake Ontario
WISCONSIN
MICHIGAN
NEW YORK
MINNESOTA
Flint
Lansing
Lake Michigan
Lake Erie
IOWA
PENNSYLVANIA
OHIO

MAP LEGEND

- ☆ Capital City
- ● City
- Michigan
- United States
- Canada
- Water

SCALE 0 — 200 Miles / 200 Kilometers

School Years

When Christopher was in fourth grade, he told his family he was going to write a book one day. They teased him, but they knew he was a good writer.

Other people also saw Christopher's potential. His teachers, in particular, found ways to encourage his talents. Miss Henry, Christopher's third grade teacher, was able to get him into a program for **gifted** students. Mr. Alums, his sixth grade teacher, was also supportive and encouraged Christopher to believe in himself.

In eighth grade, Christopher's family had to move to a new neighborhood. This meant that Christopher also had to change schools. It was difficult for him to move to a new community and school that were both 98 percent **Caucasian**.

At his new school, Christopher ran for student council. Instead of giving a speech, he wrote a song. To his surprise, he won a position on the council. It was the first time an African American had ever been elected to student council at the school.

As a child, Christopher liked to read comics more than other books. His favorites were stories about *Superman* and *Batman*.

Getting Started

High school was a time of change for Christopher. He worked at a local grocery store and mowed lawns to earn some extra money. He also started to practice his writing.

In his final year of high school, Christopher found out that he had been accepted to the University of Michigan–Flint. He needed money to help pay for school, so his father helped him get a summer job at the General Motors factory. In the fall, Christopher began his university studies.

After one year of university, Christopher decided he wanted to work at the factory full time. He made good money there. He was able to afford an apartment of his own and buy a new car.

Christopher's job took up much of his time. He worked 10-hour shifts, hanging doors on the vehicles that were being made. Whenever he had a break, he spent time practicing his writing. Christopher tried writing fiction at first, but was not happy with his work. He turned to writing about his life and experiences in the factory. This helped him come to terms with anything that upset him. It also helped the time pass more quickly.

The University of Michigan-Flint opened in 1956 as Flint Senior College. It received its current name in 1971.

Early Writing

Christopher worked in the factory for 13 years, finally leaving the job in 1985. He spent the next few years trying other types of work. Christopher also went back to university.

In 1993, he decided to submit some of his writing to the Hopwood Awards, a competition the university held for aspiring writers. To his surprise, he received two honors. An essay he wrote about working at the car factory won first prize. His story, "The Watsons Go to Florida—1963," received a second-place prize.

After winning the awards, Christopher took a year off to write. He wanted to turn his story about the Watsons into a book. Christopher decided to rename the story "The Watsons Go to Birmingham—1963." He changed the plot to draw attention to the Birmingham church bombing, a tragedy that killed four Black girls.

When the book was finished, Christopher entered it in two contests. While he did not win either award, his book caught the attention of an **editor** from Delacorte Press. She told Christopher that the company wanted to publish it.

Christopher moved to **Canada** in **1985**. He wrote his book about the **Watsons** there.

In **2000**, Christopher graduated from the **University of Michigan-Flint** with a degree in political science.

On September 15, 2013, a ceremony was held at Birmingham's 16th Street Baptist Church to commemorate the 50th anniversary of the bombing. The church had been a meeting place for people fighting for the rights of African Americans. The bombing was committed by a group who rejected these goals.

Writing Tips

Christopher put a great deal of time and effort into becoming a writer. He knows the challenges that writers face to get their work just right. Over time, he has learned what it takes to bring his ideas to life.

Write Every Day

Writing takes practice. Christopher practiced his writing every day at the factory. He still writes each day. The more writers write, the better their writing becomes. Christopher would not have become the successful writer he is today if he had not practiced his craft.

Practice Patience

Writing does not come naturally to everyone. To practice something takes patience. If something does not work, try again. It helps for writers to be patient with themselves as well. It takes time to find the style and voice that works for them. However, once they do so, their stories will become even better.

Have Fun and Enjoy the Process

Sometimes, Christopher laughs out loud when he writes or when he reads his own writing. Inventing people and places can be really fun. Writers decide what the characters do and where they go. Writers also decide what happens to them. Christopher enjoys creating his characters and taking them on a journey. When he is creating a story, he takes time to have fun and enjoy the process of writing.

Road to Success

Christopher took a big risk when he took time off to write, but his hard work paid off. *The Watsons Go to Birmingham—1963* was published in 1995. It was an immediate success. Christopher won several awards for the book. It was named a **Newbery Honor Book** and a **Coretta Scott King Award** Honor Book. These are two of the highest honors a children's writer can receive.

The accolades did not stop there. *The New York Times Book Review* and *Publishers Weekly*, two major publishing magazines, both named *The Watsons Go to Birmingham—1963* the best book of the year. It was also named to the American Library Association's Best Books for Young Adults list.

The Coretta Scott King Book Awards were created to honor authors and illustrators whose works accurately depict African American culture and values. Coretta Scott King and her husband, Martin Luther King, Jr., were noted champions of African American rights.

The success of this book encouraged Christopher to write a second one. *Bud, Not Buddy* came out in 1999. The book was special to Christopher because he had created two characters who were based on his grandfathers. His mother's father, Earl "Lefty" Lewis, had been a pitcher in the **Negro Baseball League**. Meanwhile, Herman E. Curtis, Senior, was one of the first African Americans in the United States to get his pilot's license. Christopher was proud of his grandfathers. They were leaders who helped open doors for other African Americans.

The Publishing Process

A **manuscript** goes through many stages before it is published. Often, authors change their work to follow an editor's suggestions. The final book can look very different from what the author first wrote.

Good Reads

Many of Christopher's books teach people about important periods in history. He shows readers how the past affected everyday people. The struggles of the characters in Christopher's books are as important today as they were in the past.

The Watsons Go to Birmingham—1963

Kenny's older brother, Byron, keeps getting into trouble. Their parents decide it is time to take Byron to see Grandma Sands. If anyone can set him right, she can. So, the "Weird Watsons" pack up their car, the "brown bomber," and head to Birmingham, Alabama. What starts out as a hilarious story about Kenny's daily life turns into tragedy once they arrive down South. With the support of his family, Kenny learns some valuable lessons about life and his own capabilities.

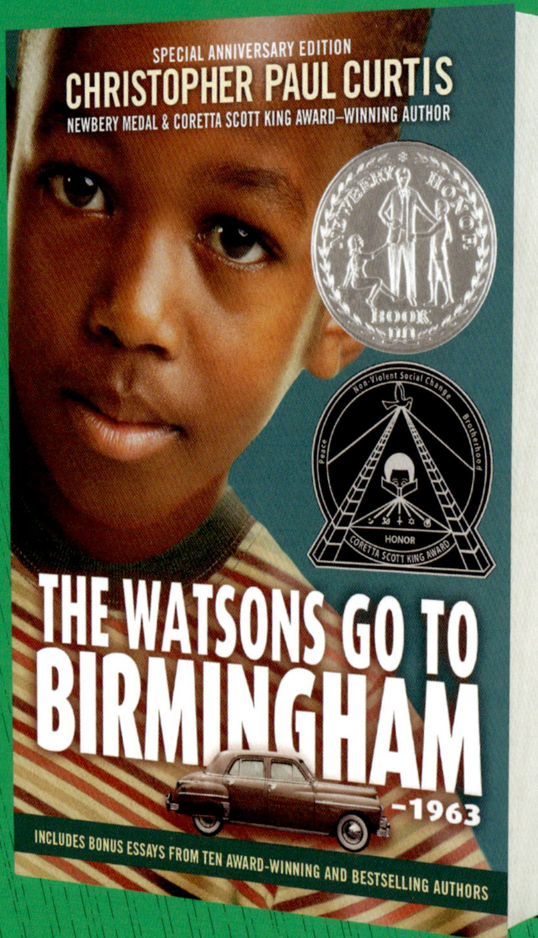

Bud, Not Buddy

Ten-year-old Bud is like hundreds of thousands of other children in the United States in 1936. He has no home, no family, and nowhere safe to live. He decides that it is time to go look for his father. Before she died, his mother left him a clue. Resourceful Bud sets out with only his suitcase and his "rules to live by." On his journey, he meets incredible characters and learns a great deal about his family and himself.

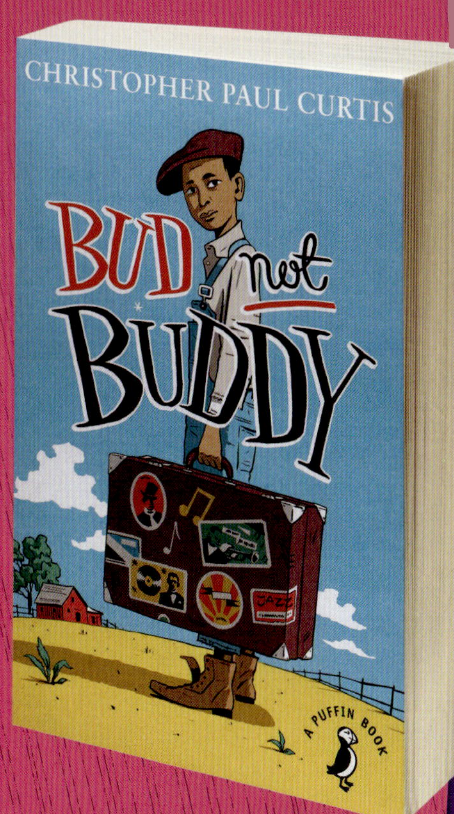

Bucking the Sarge

Fifteen-year-old Luther T. Farrell is ready to leave Flint. He is ready to go to college. He plans to become America's best-known and best-loved philosopher. He just has to win the science fair first. If he can beat Shayla Patrick, the love of his life, he might stand a chance of finding a better future.

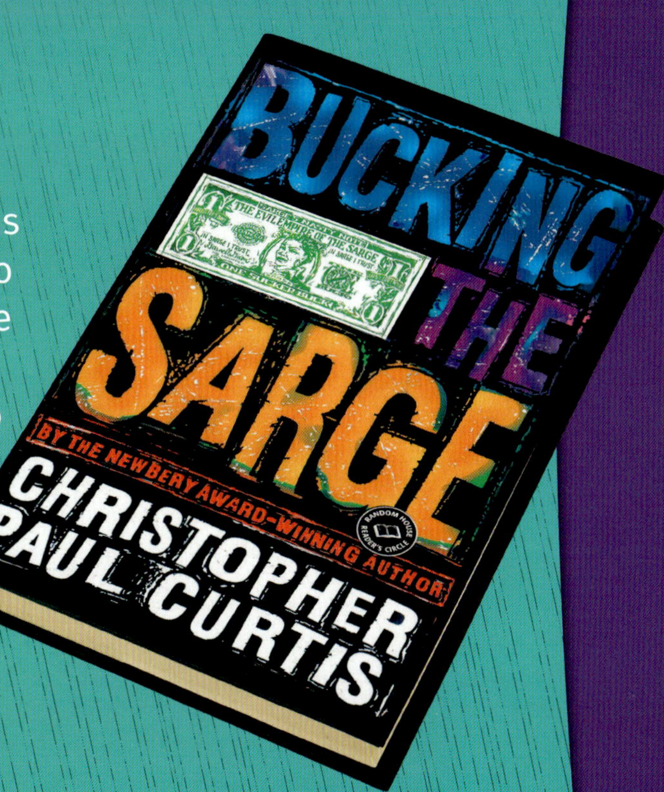

Mr. Chickee's Funny Money

Mr. Chickee gives 9-year-old Steven a funny looking bill. Could it possibly be a quadrillion-dollar bill? All Steven knows is that it has singer James Brown's face and 15 zeroes on it. Until he can figure it out, he also knows he has to keep it away from Agent Fondoo of the U.S. Treasury. Steven and his best friends, Russell and Zoopy the giant dog, do their best to hide the bill from Fondoo and his Secret Government Agents until they can determine what is going on.

The Mighty Miss Malone

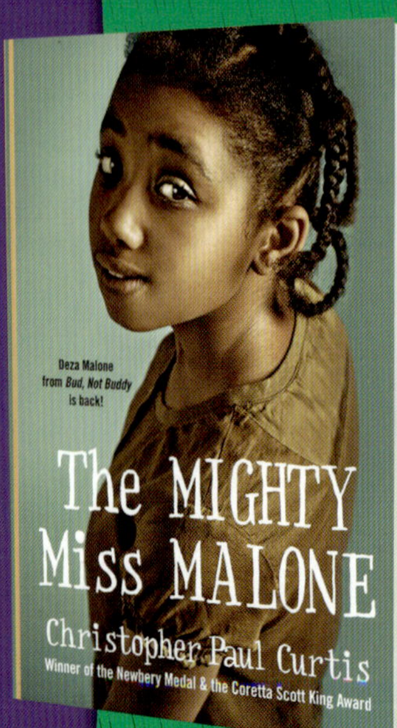

The Malone family has a motto: "We are all on a journey to this place called wonderful." Unfortunately, life during the **Great Depression** is anything but wonderful. Deza's father has left to find work. She, her mother, and her older brother Jimmie leave to find him. They end up in Hooverville, outside Flint, Michigan. Jimmie leaves to become a singer, and Deza and her mother find a new home. They still hold out hope that they will find Deza's father through all the twists and turns of their adventure.

Elijah of Buxton

The Buxton Settlement in Ontario, Canada, was an important stop on the **Underground Railroad**. It was the last stop for many slaves in search of freedom. Eleven-year-old Elijah was the first child born in the settlement. He was born free. When a former slave steals money from Elijah's friend, Elijah must help him get it back. The money was supposed to help other people escape to freedom. Elijah travels to the United States to find the thief. On his dangerous journey, he learns about slavery and the risks his parents and other slaves took to escape it.

The Madman of Piney Woods

In this novel, Christopher Paul Curtis returns to Buxton, Ontario, 40 years after Elijah's story took place. The story is told through the eyes of Benji and Red. Benji is African-Canadian, and Red is of Irish **descent**. The boys come together to uncover the mystery of the woods where they love to play. As they do, they learn many important lessons.

Milestones

Christopher's books are read around the world. His characters touch people. The subjects he writes about move them. Christopher's readers are always excited to see what he is going to write next.

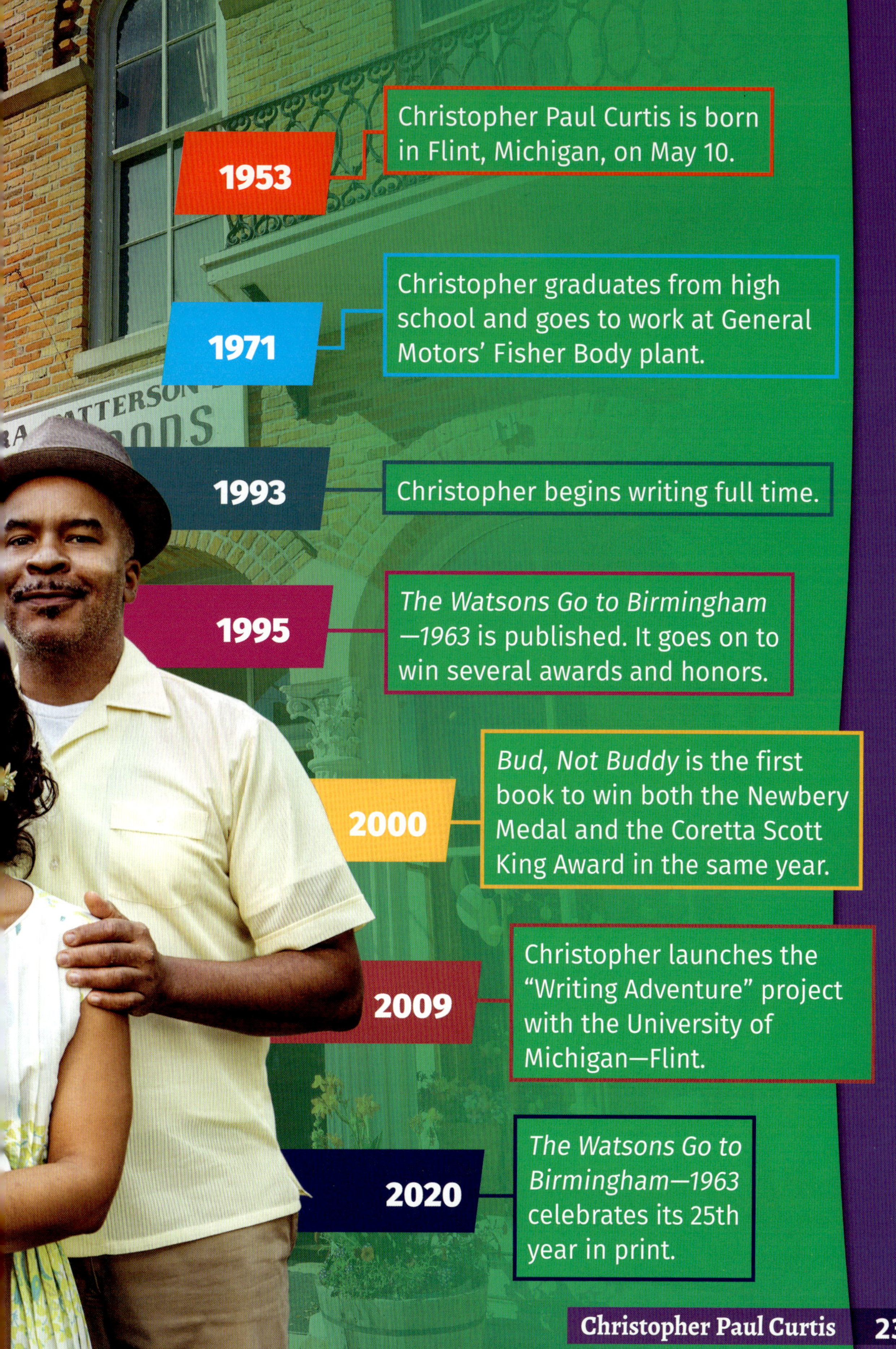

1953 Christopher Paul Curtis is born in Flint, Michigan, on May 10.

1971 Christopher graduates from high school and goes to work at General Motors' Fisher Body plant.

1993 Christopher begins writing full time.

1995 *The Watsons Go to Birmingham—1963* is published. It goes on to win several awards and honors.

2000 *Bud, Not Buddy* is the first book to win both the Newbery Medal and the Coretta Scott King Award in the same year.

2009 Christopher launches the "Writing Adventure" project with the University of Michigan—Flint.

2020 *The Watsons Go to Birmingham—1963* celebrates its 25th year in print.

Christopher Today

Christopher lives in Windsor, Ontario, Canada, with his wife, Habon Aden Curtis. They have two daughters, Ayaan and Ebyaan, and a son, Libaan. Christopher is a familiar face at the local doughnut shop and the Windsor Public Library. He does much of his writing in these two places.

The success of his first two books led Christopher to found the Nobody but Curtis Foundation. It provides books, computers, and supplies to schools and community centers that need them. The foundation also has a **scholarship** program that helps children who cannot afford a quality education.

Christopher enjoys talking with fans and aspiring writers. In 2009, he created the "Writing Adventure" project. This program provided Christopher with the opportunity to meet with young writers and give advice. Today, he often gives talks at schools and libraries. When he gives his talks, Christopher encourages young people to read. He tells them to get a library card. Christopher is a big supporter of public libraries. There, people can learn about any subject they want.

Windsor sits on the Detroit River, just across from the city of Detroit, Michigan. Windsor is a key port of entry between Canada and the United States, with an estimated $360 million worth of goods moving across the river daily.

Movies and More

In 2013, *The Watsons Go to Birmingham—1963* was made into a television movie. It was released in September of that year to coincide with the 50th anniversary of the Birmingham church bombing. Directed by Kenny Leon, the movie stars several well-known African American actors. Anika Noni Rose plays Wilona Watson, Wood Harris plays Daniel Watson, and LaTanya Richardson Jackson plays Grandma Sands. The children are played by Bryce Clyde Jenkins as Kenny, Harrison Knight as Byron, and Skai Jackson as Joetta.

Playwright Reginald André Jackson adapted *Bud, Not Buddy* for the stage. The play brings the story to life with music. Many theaters across the United States, both large and small, have staged this play.

A musical adaptation of *Mr. Chickee's Funny Money* has also appeared in theaters. The musical score was created by Lamont and Paris Dozier. Lamont wrote many of the most popular **Motown** songs in the 1960s.

Anika Noni Rose is one of today's most in-demand actresses. Besides *The Watsons Go to Birmingham*, she has also starred in numerous movies, plays, and television shows.

The Watsons Go to Birmingham was nominated for several Black Reel awards. Founded in 2000, these awards recognize the work of African American filmmakers.

Writing a Biography

All of the parts of a biography work together to tell the story of a person's life. Find out how these elements combine by writing a biography. Begin by choosing a person whose story fascinates you. You will have to research the person's life by using library books and reliable websites. If possible, you can also email the person or write him or her a letter. The person might agree to answer your questions directly.

Parts of a Biography

Early Life
- Where and when was the person born?
- What is known about the person's family and friends?
- Did the person grow up in unusual circumstances?

Growing Up
- Who had the most influence on the person?
- Did the person receive assistance from others?
- Did he or she have a positive attitude?

Developing Skills
- What was the person's education?
- What was the person's first job or work experience?
- What obstacles did the person overcome?

Early Achievements
- What was the person's most important early success?
- What processes has this person used in his or her work?
- Which of the person's traits were most helpful in his or her work?

Person Today
- Has the person received awards or recognition for accomplishments?
- What is the person's life's work?
- How have the person's accomplishments served others?

Quiz

1 Where and when was Christopher born?

2 Into how many languages have Christopher's books been translated?

3 Where did Christopher go to university?

4 Which of Christopher's books celebrated its 25th anniversary in 2020?

5 How old was Christopher when his first book was published?

6 What is the name of Christopher's foundation?

7 When was the movie *The Watsons Go to Birmingham* released?

8 For how many years did Christopher work at the General Motors plant?

ANSWERS

1. Flint, Michigan in 1953 **2.** More than 10 **3.** University of Michigan–Flint **4.** *The Watsons Go to Birmingham*—1963 **5.** 42 **6.** Nobody but Curtis Foundation **7.** 2013 **8.** 13

Author Speak

The field of writing has its own language. Understanding some of the more common writing terms will allow you to discuss your ideas about books.

action: the moving events of a story

antagonist: the person in a story who opposes the main character

autobiography: a history of a person's life, written by that person

biography: a written account of another person's life

character: a person in a story, poem, play, or other work

climax: the most exciting moment or turning point in a story

episode: a scene or short piece of action in a story

fiction: stories about characters and events that are not real

foreshadow: to hint at something that is going to happen later in a story

imagery: a written description of a thing or idea that brings an image to mind

narrator: the speaker of a story who relates its events

nonfiction: writing that deals with real people and events

novel: published writing of considerable length that portrays characters within a story

plot: the order of events in a work of fiction

protagonist: the leading character of a story

resolution: the end of a story, when the conflict is settled

scene: a single episode in a story

setting: the place and time in which a story occurs

theme: an idea that runs throughout a story

Key Words

Caucasian: having a European background

Coretta Scott King Award: an award from the American Library Association that is given to African American children's authors and illustrators whose work reflects the African-American experience

descent: the origin or background of someone in relation to family or nationality

editor: a person who revises material before publication

gifted: having exceptional talent

Great Depression: a period of economic decline that began in 1929 and lasted throughout the 1930s

manuscript: a draft of a story before it is published

Motown: rhythm and blues music from Detroit, Michigan

Negro Baseball League: an association of African American baseball teams active largely between 1920 and the late 1940s

Newbery Honor Book: an award from the American Library Association to the author of one of the year's best American children's books

scholarship: a type of financial aid given to a student

slavery: a condition in which one human being is owned by another

Underground Railroad: a network of people, African American as well as white, offering shelter and aid to escaped slaves

Index

Published by Lightbox Learning Inc.
276 5th Avenue
Suite 704 #917
New York, NY 10001
Website: www.openlightbox.com

Library of Congress Control Number: 2022947927

ISBN 978-1-7911-4836-2 (hardcover)
ISBN 978-1-7911-4837-9 (softcover)
ISBN 978-1-7911-4838-6 (multi-user eBook)

Printed in Guangzhou, China
1 2 3 4 5 6 7 8 9 0 26 25 24 23 22

102022
101321

Project Coordinator: Heather Kissock Designer: Ana María Vidal

Every reasonable effort has been made to trace ownership and to obtain permission to reprint copyright material. The publishers would be pleased to have any errors or omissions brought to their attention so that they may be corrected in subsequent printings.

The publisher acknowledges Getty Images, Alamy, Shutterstock, and Wikimedia as its primary image suppliers for this title.